The Will To Live:

Finding the Strength

Within To Survive

By

Drenda Williams

" Change can only come
by those who seek it
for themselves. "

The Will To Live: Finding The Strength Within To Survive

About the Author

Call me Chameleon. I am very shy and reserved because of my past; however, I can instantly change into a powerful woman who has not forgotten her roots and has been driven to accomplish great things relative to her beginnings. Although I sprang from a poverty-stricken childhood, I grew into a well-accomplished female executive. Being a former victim of abuse, I can't forget past traumatic situations. These terrible experiences have instilled me with a compelling need to share my story with others who suffer from abuse—or are at risk of becoming a victim of it.

I suffered through severe emotional and physical abuse that also involved my daughter and my family. It affected my life in ways I did not know until later. Writing this book is not merely something to read, it's my over-powering sense of duty to the millions of women and men who are suffering or are in great danger of suffering abuse.

The Will To Live: Finding The Strength Within To Survive has great power to me because no one was the to know what I was going through; no one was there to comfort me; no one was there to tell me what to do; no one was there to tell me what I must do to escape; no one was there because I wanted to conceal my shame and pain. Now I want to reach out and inspire young ladies—often teenagers—who need to talk to someone so they will know they are not alone in the abuse they suffer now, or are at risk of, or who have unhealed emotional wounds from past abuse.

Acknowledgements

I would first like to give all the glory to God who is the head of my life. God has been patient with me as I have grown and discovered my purpose in life. It is this purpose which leads and guides me in every aspect of my life.

To my immediate family, it wasn't always easy but I know we made the best of everything. I pray you've seen my growth, determination, and success. It wasn't just for me but to show you all that your dreams can be reality; you just have to make them so. I will always and forever love you guys!

I would like to thank my supportive circle, my Sissy DeSheila and lifelong friend Curtissa who are always there when I need a listening ear and my dear friend Jackson who pushed when I got weary. You are truly my best friends and I love you dearly for that.

To my daughters: Mayuana, Nia, and Jade...you are my blessings and it is with each day that I give my 300% to give you a better life than I had growing up. Girlies, keep

The Will To Live: Finding The Strength Within To Survive

up the good work and I expect to see even greater things from each of you. I LOVE YOU ❤

And to myself: I want to thank you for sticking with your goals and dreams. No matter how hard it was or how late you had to stay up...you did it. You have grown so much and are so resilient in this purpose-filled life. I love you just how you are for who you are and just know....... WE DID IT!!!

Overview

The Will To Live: Finding The Strength Within To Survive tells how author Drenda Williams, against all odds, escaped from abuse that started in her teen years. This set the pattern for the rest of her abusive relationship that, astonishingly, continued for some years. Her book focuses on what young women of every socio-economic background must know and do to recognize potentially abusive men and avoid or escape them. It makes its points both by relating incidents in her life but also with brief and pointed how-to-do-its. Although the target audience is teen females it is also relative to male domestic situations.

The Will To Live: Finding The Strength Within To Survive is not an academic take on the issue. Written by a woman who experienced years of abuse, it's a call to action from where the worst mistakes are made and the hardest lessons learned. *The Will To Live: Finding The Strength Within To Survive* gives teenage girls and young women most at risk of date rape and relationship abuse, the information they desperately need.

The author grew up in a very poor family in a small Missouri town. Success at school sustained her against ridicule for her family's hand-to-mouth existence. Excelling both in sports and academically, she played Varsity basketball as a starter and became her high school's first black National Honor Society President. Scholarships enabled her to attend and graduate from college cum laude. Her work as an intern while in college allowed her to convert the internship into a full time career with the federal government. She has repeatedly been promoted for her meritorious work there.

Her continuous drive, accomplishments, and purpose is a testament that through tragedy there is always a lesson to learn.   That lesson provides a pathway to personal growth and doesn't define your future but allows you to serve as a testimony of victory to others.

TABLE OF CONTENTS

The Will To Live: Finding The Strength Within To Survive

Introduction

In the beginning, when I really decided to focus on myself and to strengthen those qualities which were weak at that time; it was then when I found out what my purpose was. I was here to support those who have no voice, to strengthen those who are weak, and to fight for those causes which make a difference even if it is just for one person. I realized how fortunate I was to survive domestic violence. I knew it wasn't by mistake.

There was a reason and it was then that I began to figure out who and what I could do so I decided to share my story not only to recount the events that took place but to list those events and provide guidance to those currently dealing with domestic violence. I wanted to offer the little voice in your head which confirms what you may or may not want to believe and this is how my book came about. It is to show someone else has been through the same situation you are or have been in, and how by the grace and blessings of God I made it through. There were things I could have done and things I shouldn't have done so I don't take the recognition of those things for granted. These lessons are being shared

The Will To Live: Finding The Strength Within To Survive

in the hopes of inciting the strength you need to get through or to provide others who may be looking inside the situation from the outside an idea of what happens in these situations, how can they help, and the thought process of someone being abused.

Much has happened in my life and although there were negative things, God saw fit to provide so many other positive things to keep me going and never giving up. So I ask of you if you are reading this in the hopes of finding encouragement to make it through, you will get that; but you will also get a powerful story of a young girl who transformed into a woman who didn't let the darkness of her past affect the potential of her future. I would like to start with a paper my oldest daughter wrote when she was 16 years old. It is touching and I felt it was the best way to start this book because she was a survivor of domestic violence by being a child affected by these events, but like me she found the strength to progress and so now your journey begins.................................

Mayuana Hutt

English III

Mrs. Cooper

September 1, 2011

My twin, My inspiration

According to dictionary.com, bravery is described, "as courage and valor." Not everyone can be classified as brave, but when you are, people look up to you. This is why I look up to my mom. A person would have to be very brave and strong to become successful after experiencing the traumatic events life has brought upon me and my mother. I've learned how to face life and hardships with a smile and know that you can be successful no matter what. It's about your effort. My

14

mom is inspirational; she is so many great things. She has great positive hobbies. My mother gives effort and can do anything, become anything, be anything.

From culinary artist to stylish shoe fashionista, my mother is a chic, swanky chef. She loves to whip up extravagant cuisines. Our kitchen always has a diverse smell, from scallops dressed in tangy pineapple sauce to crisp homemade apple pie. Numerous cookbooks by her favorite chefs crowd our counters and refrigerator top. The recipes are endless. Her movements are swift and busy. She constantly maneuvers through spices and herbs as if she were a sly snake slithering threw the jungle, clothed in her apron, with the name of her favorite New Orleans café boasted across the front. All of the burners are occupied as my mother frantically cooks many parts to her one sublime dish. I love to see my mother like this; she's so happy and child-like. It amazes me how content she is after all we've been through.

A lot of people dislike feet. They can't stand to look, touch, or even talk about feet. My mom is not one of these people. She loves her feet and takes pride in her toes. Pedicures are weekly; colors of the rainbow ribbon

15

themselves onto my mother's toes. You would wonder why she keeps her toes so sassy. I would have to say because of her shoes. There is a vast amount; from wedges to peep-toe heels. They are like an ancient king's crowns; she has so many. They are stacked, high as a mountain. Each day she climbs this mountain to find the perfect pair that both matches her outfit and displays her fresh pedicure; variety is the key. She takes pride in her shoes and her toes. She is so confident. It's astounding knowing what she's endured on those feet. Her story could inspire others.

There are so many events that I could tell about my mom, but one stays vaguely familiar. It was a late night about 13 years ago when I was about 3. I sat on my mom's bed in Vandalia, MO. I was just like every three year-old, oblivious to the world, but something put my life in perspective. With fear in her voice my mom said, "May, go put on some clothes so we can leave." Me, being the know-it-all three year-old proceeded to say, "Why Mom? It is too late to go anywhere!" She told me some bad people were coming, and I needed to hurry up. I was so scared, I rushed to put on some clothes, we got into the car, and drove to my grandma's. Vandalia is a

The Will To Live: Finding The Strength Within To Survive

fairly small town, so it didn't take long to get to my grandparent's house.

Shortly after we parked and got out another car came; we ran to the door. I got in the house but I remember my mom was outside. I looked out the door to see my dad; I can't remember correctly, but he might have had a gun. He was yelling, cussing, and threatening her. I was so scared. There were a bunch of big guys in dark clothes with him.

My grandpa came outside and just stood there, I thought it was to make sure my dad didn't hit my mom. It seemed like hours, and my dad still didn't let her go. I remember my uncle sneaking out the back door so he could go get the cops; eventually they showed up. I was so thankful for my uncle. That was just one out of many times my dad had this behavior. To think that my mom could go through that and be successful, she's the XXXXX XXXXXXXXXX for the state of Missouri, astounds me. I think people could become successful no matter what. Even to this day I wonder what would've happen if we wouldn't have left our apartment. Would we even be alive?

The Will To Live: Finding The Strength Within To Survive

The previous passages described how confident, happy, brave, strong, and successful my mother is. I look up to her, in her high-heels. She, to me, is a majestic noble of esteem. I've learned to embrace your talents to the fullest and to "always give 300%." Witnessing and hearing about her struggles can give you a new perspective on life. It makes you think about complaining and cherishing the small things in life. My mom is a great person. I'm so grateful to have her. She has made me a stronger woman!

Chapter 1 ~ Learn From My Mistakes

Yes, learn from my mistakes. If you don't, you're likely to repeat them. Repeating them will often mean that a wonderful period of your life should be among your happiest times will turn into a miserable struggle for survival where the odds are stacked against you.

It was the day that changed my life. I remember it so vividly. Sometimes I would fall into his trap. Always seeing the good in things would come back to haunt me. I was being nice and brought our daughter to visit him. Back then he didn't help take care of her so any small amount of time was meaningful to me and I

19

wanted her to know her father, but what appeared to be such an innocent visit turned out to be a big mistake.

It started out with no drama or arguments. We would go for a drive just to have a talk about our relationship—my thoughts were maybe things would get better. Our daughter would be left with grandma so we wouldn't have any interruptions. I left without knowing what was in store for me. We drove down the windy black top. In the country there are always quiet places you can pull over to sit and talk. I wasn't sure where we were going but I felt like probably to his friend's house.

After a certain point the turn was unfamiliar; it was a left turn off a sharp curve. Where were we going? I took the turn and we parked by a metal shed. To this day I remember how it looked. The grass was browning and there was no farmstead out there just an isolated shed near the road.

When I turned the engine off, he told me that he wanted sex. I told him, "No, it's not like that anymore and no, I don't what to." He started cussing out of anger because of my response and I saw him get in the glove box. He

20

was always in a rage when he went there so this time I didn't know what was going to happen and at this point I was afraid. Before I knew it I had a gun pointed to my head. He yelled, "Now say no!" The tone of his comments were full of anger. I had never seen a real gun and at this point, with it pointed at my temple, I began to cry. I was so scared and all I could do was pray that he didn't pull the trigger. So much went through my head: Was I going to see my mom? What about my daughter? I was not ready to die at twenty-two. I just prayed that I would get out of this situation.

He got out of the car with the gun and came around to the driver's side. His whole plan was to have me drive to this location so he could control me. Maybe it was a game to him; I don't know. He stepped to the driver's side and pointed the gun at me and told me to get out of the car. At this time, I felt like I had no option but to concede and have sex with him if I were to live. I was in the country, no one was around, no one would hear me, no one would see me, and no one could help me. I remember being on my cycle; although, he didn't care. I remember being raped outside in the country. I will never forget that road, the shed, the car, the gun, and the pain.

21

Once he finished, we got back into the car. No words were exchanged. Nothing, not a word. How could he be so cold? Such a monster to do such a thing and then sit there emotionless.

We came back to his house and I got our daughter. I was hurt and I was broken. I decided I needed to do what I knew I had to do. Still shaken, I drove to the hospital. It was not too far, maybe five miles or so. I was violated and I wasn't going to allow him to do this to me.

I got there and they put me in an exam room. I remember an officer being there. Still shaken and after completing the rape kit, I heard a familiar voice. It was him! He was there! I could hear him walk down the hall to the room. They even allowed him to come to my hospital room. I was screaming uncontrollably and hysterically because of the rape at gun point and for him to come to the hospital made me frightened. I told them he had a gun but by that time he must have hidden it. What I remember out of that incident was the rape kit, the police report, and to this day, nothing has happened.

The Will To Live: Finding The Strength Within To Survive

There was another time I recall that traumatized me a lot. It was a time where he put me out of his house over something petty. I had gone down the street to visit a friend. Jealousy had controlled him so he called me to come back for a brief talk. Again, not wanting to believe the angry person he showed me he could be, I went and he started getting upset—so upset and violent that he took my head and hit it on the metal bunk beds. It's still so vivid. How it felt when my head near the temple area hit the screws; not the smooth metal part, but the part that contained the screws which held the rails to the bunk. It was the first time I had a huge protrusion on the side of my head. The knot was the size of a golf ball and the black eye was severe. I was so scared of the laceration on my temple that I called for a ride to the ER. They did an MRI and I had a concussion. For weeks I had to live with that decision to go back and talk to him.

Then there was the car chase. It was night and I was in the town of my abuser. Our young daughter was in the back seat. I can't remember why he was upset but what I remember was fearing for our lives as he chased us at full speed down the streets of the city.

23

I had to make a drastic decision that day.....cross over a highway not knowing if I could make it across before I got side swiped. I couldn't stop because he would ram me or block me off from escaping. We were spared that day but when would the next incident occur? When would I learn? When would I believe him to be the person he showed me he was? These episodes were just a few of many in which was the darkness I lived through for seven years.

Chapter 2 ~ How It All Began

Childhood can be a very difficult period in a person's life.
The truth of the matter is, kids are mean. Growing up
was rough for me and even though I made it through
those years, the emotional scars and hurt stuck with me
for many years.

I came from a family with three siblings living in the
home. Our mother worked at a factory job and provided
the family's sole income through most of my childhood.
She didn't have extra money most times so we wore
garage sale clothes, donations, or hand me downs. Many
times we did without. Now you may think this means no

designer jeans, no trips to the mall, no eating out at restaurants and so on. No, I'm talking about getting along without necessities like water, food, shelter, heat, and electricity.

We grew up very poor but still blessed because we always had a place to live. Our homes may not have been in the best condition but at least we had one. I always had to share a room. Keeping warm, having clean clothes, and food were daily concerns. In the small town of Vandalia African Americans typically lived on the south side of town. We lived next to the brickyard on the outskirts of town. It seemed like all the houses we lived in started off as fully functioning homes, but their reclaimed fixtures soon gave us constant trouble and in a short time some of the plumbing stopped working and the houses all lost the battle against mice and roaches.

When you are young you shouldn't have to worry about food, but it was always a concern. Sometimes we had it; sometimes we didn't. Back then you had food stamp coupons to use at the store but they were not as concealable as today's EBT (Electronic Benefit Transfer) or SNAP cards. Some days we had to do without much to

26

eat; sometimes it was a slice of bread or instant potatoes. At the thinnest times, it was just water to make your stomach feel full. I always wondered why we had pets if we didn't even have food for ourselves but those pets did bring some happiness into our lives.

Being picked on was the norm. Not realizing the long-term effect it has, my peers often jeered, laughed and whispered about our living conditions. Luckily by high school my mom managed to get financing for a mobile home giving the appearance of some financial gain. After an introductory period the payments ballooned, a scam she didn't know. The mobile home was repossessed to the amusement of my classmates.

Years of this torment from the first grade on took its toll. My self-esteem diminished to little or nothing. I hated who I was and what I had become. My lack of a strong feeling of self-worth developed in elementary school and spanned into my twenties. In the meantime I told my mother I wanted to be another race and despised her for the conditions we were raised in—as if it were her fault. She didn't plan on being the only income source. I realize now she did her best and worked herself hard through a

27

stressful and deprived life until all her children were old enough to take care of themselves.

My mother is a strong woman who did the best she could having lost her mother while she was still in high school. I'm blessed to have her. She is strong, caring, and selfless. My mother was able to raise three children all of which went to college and two have graduated as 1st generation college students in our family.......I'm so proud of her.

My escape was school. I had nothing but school. It was my safe haven in spite of the mental torture I had to endure from the other kids. The system allowed me to focus on school work and to some extent it blocked out the constant reminders and taunts thrown at me that I was a nobody. I didn't have anything else, but I did get good grades. I'm now convinced this long-continued harassment was the main factor leading me to jump at the chance to be my abuser's girlfriend. Even though he didn't excel at academics, he was a star at sports. He was known around the state and looking back at it now, made me feel important.

Although I didn't know it then, staying focused on doing well in school was the blessing that ultimately got me through. It was my escape from the years of being torn down to nothing and my escape route from years of abuse. Obtaining the knowledge to develop and grow myself would ultimately be the one thing that would build me up to what I am today.

The Will To Live: Finding The Strength Within To Survive

Chapter 3 ~ The Journey

This most important lesson I learned was you need to love yourself. Although everyone goes through trials, some of us have to endure more than others. Know that God created all of us equally; no one is more or less important than anyone else. If you don't love the person who exists within you, no one will. In many ways self-respect and self-love are the same. If you have one, you also have the other. Cultivate those qualities. In some people, me for example, respect and love of self was a wilted flower that refused to grow for many years, allowing me to be led through a life of misery and a seven-year span of abuse that nearly killed me.

Sometimes young women and especially teens allow their feelings of self-worth to be tied to keeping a male in their lives because they believe it makes them somebody. However, a man does not make you better than you make yourself. You are an independent individual, responsible for your own happiness, success, and those vital feelings of self-worth.

How many people suspect this important aspect of a human being's feeling of self-worth would have so much control over how a person maneuvers through life? Many of the choices you make have long-range consequences. You cannot expect others to treat you with high regard if internally you believe you're worth nothing. Not only do you think it but you act it. When those who prey on the weak get wind of it—and many of them can read you with a glance—they know how to twist your emotional needs to further their purpose.

I didn't know until I began this book journey the answer is a simple two-word principle which can make all the difference. It is *love yourself*. You are worthy no matter

The Will To Live: Finding The Strength Within To Survive

what you have experienced. Two entities of vast importance in your life always love you . . . God and you!

Self-love is so valuable. Its positive qualities exist in all of us. They are mixed with another powerful element; memories of past mistakes, failures, and shortcomings. The vital thing is to stir the mix so that self-love always comes to the top.

I was always in school because it gave me things to be proud of. I made straight A's. In tenth grade I played basketball and got some attention for playing on Varsity as a starter. I excelled in track. School became my passion and my hobby because there was no money for anything else. I started accomplishing things and that fired my determination to do more.

I earned a lot of basketball recognition and for track as well. My name was in the paper for games. Life was good, except for the really vicious physical abuse that started in my junior year. I think he was upset because he had a full ride to college but wouldn't go. He blamed me. He thought if he didn't go, I wouldn't either. He was wrong. I applied for a federal scholarship and got it so I

The Will To Live: Finding The Strength Within To Survive

was held in high regard by the community and school. I graduated in the top 10% of my class with a full ride to college and a paid internship with the federal government. I felt he resented me because it meant I was pulling ahead of him.

After I graduated from high school, I didn't want to be under my parents' thumb all the time because they were strict. Looking back, I know things would have gone much better for me if I had lived by their rules until I got older. Instead, I did something I still find hard to believe; I moved in with my abuser and his family until I left for college. It was the bit of freedom I wanted. Big mistake. Big, big mistake.

Although I was on my own, there was no way I was not going to college. I wanted a better life for myself. When I received the scholarship upon graduating from high school at the age of 17, I immediately became a federal employee with permanent employment upon college graduation. This meant I had a paying job. A good starting salary to help me take care of myself.

34

I also played college basketball as a walk-on. The love I had for the sport in high school carried over into my college years. I didn't need an athletic scholarship because I had a full academic scholarship. When I had a chance to come play for the coach in the summer prior to enrollment, I was selected for the team. These activities still kept me somewhat focused despite of the abuse I endured I was an 18 year old college freshman.

The abuse got worse after I started college. He hid my college textbooks from me. I cried because I didn't have any books. Sometimes he would drop in at college and fight me in front of people. I tried to stay away from him but he would just pop up. I was sexually active with him and not being raised to know about birth control and sex, I was with child during the summer after my freshman year. I continued school up until the end of my sophomore fall semester because the baby was due in the winter of 1995.

I stayed with his family off and on until after our daughter was delivered in February. After the birth I was in the hospital for a week because I kept a high fever. My parents came and his mother came. He only came a few times to the hospital for a few minutes. I knew then I needed to go home to my parents. I lived with them until I went back to college in the fall to begin the last part of my sophomore year of college. Even though I had a child and had two and a half years of college left to complete, I was still determined to finish school and obtain a degree.

Learning came easy to me. I am not sure why but I have a dynamic, almost photographic, memory for things I read and see. I spent my nights taking care of our daughter, working part time, and studying. If it wasn't for this gift, it would have been harder for me to graduate cum laude. When you are determined and focused, you are able to make the best of all situations.

Reflecting back on it now, I could have lost my scholarship because I only sat out a semester to have the baby but someone was rooting for me. The lady who fought for me to keep my scholarship is now a great friend of mine. I sat out one semester, kept a job at the local Dairy Queen I had worked at in high school, and got back to where I needed to be. I worked at Dairy Queen in high school and they hired me back when I was sitting out

The Will To Live: Finding The Strength Within To Survive

from college. During that time I stayed with my parents. Sometimes I would drive down so he could see our daughter but she wasn't his focus. He would take my car and I would have a hard time getting to work. I managed though. He would only see his daughter when I took her to him. Basically he wasn't an active father to our child and for the most part nonexistent.

He tried to make it impossible for me to keep going to college. It was a constant struggle. One time he poured bleach on all my clothes and I didn't have many. He wouldn't even keep our daughter so I would miss class. Deep down I'm sure he knew I was destined for a better life than he could achieve. That idea made him furious. He wanted me to be complacent with the life I left behind. All this drama and I was still doing my best to go to college as a single parent at the age of 20.

I was very vulnerable at that time. Caring for a baby alone and doing well in college left little time to earn money. So weekends when I went home the only way I could get money for things the baby needed was to take money from his pockets because he didn't help. I'd leave most of it so he'd be less likely to notice; I knew he didn't keep close track of how much he had. I didn't think it was stealing; after all he was the baby's father. I only did this when he was sleeping from drinking. It was my only means of help; a sad option but I had to do it.

Once he caught me pulling money out of the pants he'd thrown on the floor before flopping on the bed. I was short of time and moved before he was sound asleep. He jumped up, pushed me, and took the money back. I was a lot more careful after that but I kept on taking money from him when I needed it for the baby. He never caught me a second time, which is good because he would have given me a serious beating.

During the abuse in college I did confide in a friend. We both had a part-time job as part of a cleaning crew. We didn't have a relationship beyond being friends but he knew some of my horror stories and even got involved. He would always walk me home from work because I had to go through a not-so-good neighborhood. He even went so far as to take up for me by asking my abuser, "What's the problem?" one night. My abuser sputtered and walked away.

Right after that he beat me because he took what my friend said as a challenge. He was quick to beat on a woman; but slow about taking on a man unless he had to. I understand that's typical; the cowardly men who abuse women are usually afraid of other men unless they use liquid courage which he often had. The last time I saw him; he had been fighting while drunk and came out of it with a broken arm.

When our daughter was three, one time I told him to help take care of her. "Find her a dad," he snarled. Coming from him, that didn't ring true; he was always jealous and vindictive if he thought I was interested in another man. But of course he always wanted everything both ways.

That was the last time I took her to see him. He never sent money or came to see her. He was in and out of prison. When our daughter was in high school he was out and on parole. He had a job that provided $65 per week—child support. The same amount as the child support amount set twelve years before when he was not working.

Meanwhile, I graduated from Lincoln University cum laude and went to work full time with the government but I still had drama to deal with. It was a blessing to still be able to continue my education even though I had to take care of another life. I remember my study time was between midnight and 3 am but I did what I had to do in order to succeed. Upon graduation, I moved back home. I spent a lot of my free time running back to my abuser's hometown to hang out with friends and unbeknownst to me, this always involved enduring abuse. Since the towns were 30 miles apart, moving back wasn't the best option.

So much time had went by. The friend I met in college came back into my life. We got married and had 2 children, wonderful girls. I learned a lot during that time. I had a lot of healing and personal growth to do. I got married at 28 and it was too young looking back on it now. As previously stated I started learning my purpose at 25 so throwing a husband and more kids into the mix wasn't ideal for my situation...another lesson learned.

There were arguments and times when it wasn't a good situation for us. One thing I took away from the past's lesson was when you see signs, don't ignore them. As an individual single or married, you can't be subjected to your partners' deficiencies causing them to mentally, emotionally, and/or physically abuse you. I value the sacred institute of marriage but not at the expense of breaking my spirit. It was time for me to end it. I had learned probably around the 5th year. It was a different type of abuse.

This time around my relationship with God was different. Looking back on it now, was it a test to see if I had learned the lesson? During this situation, I prayed for wisdom and an answer in this situation from God on what to do. See God allowed me to learn from these two very different yet similar situations in order to be able to have a testimony to tell others. Don't ever let someone break your spirit; not your boyfriend, husband, family member, or yourself.

I thank God for keeping me throughout my life. This book is not only to help others but will also help others to understand me. I've been through a lot but I am not cold or bitter. I've learned valuable lessons and use those to make a difference in the lives of others. Many dark

41

secrets have never been communicated to anyone. One thing about God the timing of things is always right and I feel there is no better time than this to open up my world because even my own family doesn't know half of what I endured.

I'm a hard worker. I care about doing the right thing and helping others. It's what I take with me into my professional life. I give 300% and it has allowed me to achieve what I consider to be great success, especially considering where I came from and how rough the road I traveled was. My hard work can be attributed to my mother who worked hard to give us the little we had.

So although these tragic things occurred you would never know by my daily walk, talk, and service. As the wounds have healed my past hasn't dictated my future. I didn't ask to be put in a position on a daily basis to be in a position to give light to so many people it was just God's plan and I wear it proudly.

Now after sharing a glimpse into my life it's time to provide some helpful guidance by showing additional pieces of my life and what those being abused can do

42

when you are in a weak state where you question, and you blame yourself, or you blame others. The remainder of the book will be answers to those voices that question, doubt, or are too weak to make the choices needed to make it though. I ask for one thing and that is to listen with an open heart because it will speak to you only if you listen.

The Will To Live: Finding The Strength Within To Survive

Chapter 4 ~ My Big, Big Mistake

Now I call myself a beautiful spirit, but I didn't always feel
that way. Back then I mostly felt deprived. All the girls in
my classes dressed better than I could—a lot better. I
wore hand-me-downs that had seen hard wear from
someone else. It seemed like the other girls were always
showing off something their parents had just given them.
They'd look at me, knowing I wasn't ever going have a
new bracelet or watch to show off. Some of the girls
gloated, some looked at me sympathetically. My poverty
was embarrassing to me, and made me angry....why
me.......what did I do? I understood this better, years
later. At the time it just hurt badly.

So along comes "him", the neighboring school's star athlete, and to my amazement he pays some attention to the hurting girl I was then. He was my first and only boyfriend in high school. Now I know I was a prize to him; but he knew also right off that he could dominate me. I wasn't smart enough about men to know how to seize the upper hand. (How could I be? He was my only boyfriend.) The plain truth is I needed him far more than he needed me. He was stringing several other girls along at the same time so I knew I had my work cut out to hold him. Now I am older I realize he wasn't all that attractive in spirit. It was a beauty and the beast kind of story. I was good and he was evil so if he could have me it was like getting a trophy. He didn't smoothly and gently seduce me—a rather laughable idea concerning someone as self-centered as he was. He needed trophies and successes; he had average grades and realized he had to capitalize on his athleticism.

Three major factors led me to staying with him: first, I was afraid of him. Second, my low self-esteem and third, crippling lack of self-love left me emotionally needful to a desperate degree. I saw him as someone who cared about me but just did bad things. I kept trying to

46

rationalize why it was okay for him to be cruel to me. I was afraid he would kill me so I was like his little puppet. I felt he made me do what he said and what he wanted. If I said anything against it I would get beaten or scared just enough to make me fall in line. Those years of being poor and picked on hurt and played a big part in keeping me in this situation.

He was basically the first guy who ever showed me attention—so I was easy pickings for him. I knew it wasn't normal to be treated the way he did but when in that situation, I didn't have enough self-esteem to break away. I remember going to the prom with my cousins because only one guy who wasn't family asked me. But he only did because he wanted sex and when he found out I wasn't going to do it, he asked another girl. Hurtful times, I tell you.

So when his attention turned negative and became harmful, it was still attention. When you are at your lowest point, harmful attention may seem better than no attention at all. I think now about how I was treated, it's sickening. I am so much better than that. I am blessed I wasn't brought down to such a low level I could never

The Will To Live: Finding The Strength Within To Survive

bounce back. If I'd had more self-love or was used to being treated with respect, I wouldn't have been afraid and wouldn't have allowed myself to be treated like dirt. How people viewed me is what I internalized. I remember him calling me trash—just because I was poor. He made it seem like no one wanted me and he was doing me a favor to pay any attention to me at all. If you internalize you are nobody you'll allow yourself to be treated as nobody. Part of the abuse syndrome is self-centered men have a tough guy aura some women and girls find irresistible, thus setting themselves up for a life of misery. Happiness can't exist without self-love.

What brought me to my low point with him was not having a man in my life to show me love, and to help me understand about relationships. My real father wasn't there; however, my stepfather was in my life since I was one years old. I think even though there is a father figure in your life, you can still be missing something. What I was missing was the feeling of being wanted and loved by my father. The absence of that love allowed him to come in and fill the void even though he lacked every quality and emotion it takes to be a loving male.

The Will To Live: Finding The Strength Within To Survive

I have learned a lot about relationships since then. He was my only high school boyfriend if you want to stretch definition of that term to its breaking point. In my day we didn't have sex education in school. My parents sheltered us in the weird but widespread belief that keeping us totally ignorant about sex was the best way to prevent us from being harmed by sex. As a result, I was naive about a lot of stuff.

Before the rape, I was a virgin. The whole sex thing was a mystery to me. Society has changed enormously from what it was just twenty years ago—between the internet and TV, today's kids know more about sex by the time they're eight than I did at sixteen. After the rape I remember I would go to his home and he would take me to the attic only to have sex. I didn't want it but after I knew he would take it anyway, all of my cries were internal. I would be kind of numb wondering why he did it. He was promiscuous while we had a sexual relationship. At the time I welcomed his promiscuity because it meant fewer trips to the attic.

If I said anything about his other escapades he would get angry whether we were alone or were in front of

49

everyone. He didn't care. His family always told me it was my fault for "getting him riled up." That was just an excuse; none of his family dared interfere. It was as if they condoned it or ignored. Everyone seemed to be afraid of him—for good reason. Even before he was fully grown they'd seen how violent he was becoming. He grew up thinking violence was the answer because it was the only thing that worked for him.

I on the other hand was raised in a more controlled manner. My parents wanted me to follow their rules. I got tired of being held to strict standards. Why couldn't I go with friends, walk to the store, and have fun? It was always what they wanted and how they wanted us to do it. There was no freedom. I moved in with him because it was the only place I could have some sense of freedom. When you live with your parents it's by their rules and I felt some were excessive.

I would consider my upbringing strict. We knew right from wrong—what to do and what not to do. The flaw in that kind of training is, we were never allowed to find out about things for ourselves. When I had to make some choices for myself, I was afraid to. With him, I was a follower, not a leader, because I had never been allowed to lead myself.

That's another big difference between me back then and me today. Now I am a leader. I try to instill that characteristic with my children: make the right decisions and don't follow something or someone you know is wrong. If you love yourself, you will have the confidence to say I can do this, I will do this, and I won't do that. Being a leader is not always easy but when you know things based on your own knowledge and experiences, it's useful. I've learned leading is one of my gifts and I use my leadership for my purpose.

Chapter 5 ~ Recognize the Signs of Oncoming Abuse Before It Starts

"You always say it won't happen to me! If that was me.....I would do this.....Why does she stay?" You always have a voice of reason when we are the third party in the situation. One thing is for certain taking our own advice outside of a situation is much easier than when we are in it. I started out the same way. Growing up watching Lifetime where you always see the abuse story where you ask yourself why? Why? Why? It's so easy but without that inner soul that is ready to exhibit the survival of the fittest mode one begins to question their strength, inner peace, worth of self, and some things that seem like common sense.

What becomes the most important thing in a domestic violence situation are the signs. What are signs you may ask? They are behaviors and characteristics someone exhibits, whether they are aggressive, anger induced, or neither. During any interactions you can get a feel for a person by your interaction. Even if they don't show initially they will always come out the more time you spend with someone.

Sometimes we try to rationalize behaviors and make excuses for why others do them. Maybe they were just upset? Did I irritate them? It won't happen again. You can never rationalize abuse and if you do, something is wrong with your way of thinking.

As I look over the time I spent in an abusive relationship there were so many signs and they went noticed just ignored. One thing is they may not start out violent. Most times they start inconsistent but then get consistent and very violent. This was my experience with the signs.

In the beginning there were no signs at all but then later I began to notice the jealous behaviors turned into controlling behaviors. Some examples were being thrown

The Will To Live: Finding The Strength Within To Survive

on the hood of a car. Just for the mere thought of me talking to someone I knew in the gas station. The continuous urge for him to always get into fights. It was more than protecting himself it was something about the urge to always have the upper hand so everyone would know of the victories.

Why didn't I pay attention? It seemed as if he was like that with others but when he did it to me it was a bit of a shock like how did this happen. After the shock left it was more of a guilty feeling like I did something, knowing I didn't do a thing. It was as if I had to rationalize a behavior that wasn't mine.

Later on it got worse. It was the punching, the dragging, the threatening, and then stalker-type behavior. When it got worse that's when fear was used. If I was afraid of him then I wouldn't go. It worked but what is surprising looking back on it now, it wasn't just me who was afraid, it was a community.

Their family was known for their violent behavior—it spanned over generations. Even my mother knew of some of the family's run-ins as she was friends with

The Will To Live: Finding The Strength Within To Survive

older generations. Is this behavior genetic? I don't know but what I did know is I watched him fight other men and sometimes their family fought women. Can violence be a learned behavior? I don't know but what I do know is I had enough warnings and can only blame myself.

My abuser had some reason for exhibiting these signs but I will never know why. I don't bother to ask as I know unconsciously and consciously we have behaviors and when given much effort they can be eliminated. Did I have to go through everything I did? No! Did he get enjoyment out of it? Or was it his own deficiencies that caused him to act in such a manner? I will never know.

So when pushes and grabs turned to punches and lacerations...I should have took action. When the violence always ended with I'm sorry or I love you...I should have noticed. When the stalking started and the control by fear was the daily norm I noticed but by then I had gotten myself in a situation so entrenched with abuse it felt as if I was hopeless. After it was all said and done the first incident should have been the last.

Later on in life I noticed signs in my marriage instead of enduring the extent of what I had done in my high school relationship I didn't ignore the signs. The nature of them were different but yet the same. With any situation there are always lessons and I had learned this time. If you can go zero to a hundred and act as if you've done nothing wrong something isn't right. So before I ended up in a situation I already knew the outcome of, I left.

No matter what you are going through or what you have gone through you should always take away a lesson. I take the lessons with me everywhere I go in life. I recognize signs and it is not always abusive behavior but it could even be negative energy or characteristics I chose to not be associated with. This sign recognition is a life saver because if I didn't learn the lesson I would probably continue to make excuses for behaviors I know aren't right. So my advice to you is when you see a sign it means something and don't ignore it because you may never see another sign again because by then it would be too late.

The Will To Live: Finding The Strength Within To Survive

The Will To Live: Finding The Strength Within To Survive

Chapter 6 ~ You Have To Help Yourself

When you don't know what to do you look for others to help. It's as if you have no strength and courage unless someone believes in you. All the confidence you once had has diminished by the broken spirit you've come to accept. The first thing you want to do is ask for help...someone who will listen to the problem and sympathize with you. You look for this person to provide some sort of consoling and maybe even some options on how you should get out of a domestic violence situation. You are searching wanting to make a change but need someone to help you. A co-signer will help carry the burden of being abused. They will sit with you through it all but one thing they can't do is change your situation and end the abuse, nor can they get you out.

When I thought I could handle this situation myself I never said anything nor called for help. It was when the situation got worse and I couldn't fix it that I called for help. Help from who? I would ask those standing by to help me. I would call the police to help me. Most importantly I called on my family to help me but was I ready for that help? I don't think I was.

One time I remember missing college finals my freshman year. I went to visit my abuser. He may have picked me up because at that time I had no car I remember staying at his parents. He decided he wasn't going to take me back to school which was 2 hours away. I am sure it was intentional. The school became worried. Teachers were calling my parents. One day the county sheriff deputy showed up at the door. I thought this was my saving grace because I had made several pleas to be taken back to school so I wouldn't miss my finals. Apparently my parent's reported me missing. The odd thing was they didn't come get me after that day and the deputy didn't take me. He was there to make sure I was alive I guess.

I needed my family. I needed them to take me back to school but the lesson I learned that day...you can only depend on yourself. This made it even harder to think I could make it out because my mind was still my own worst enemy.

What is it which causes this internal weakness? Is it lack of a strong faith in God that all things are possible? Is it lack of confidence due to acknowledgement of weaknesses but no plan on how to strengthen them? One verse I never used during my years of being a domestic abuse victim until I got through my abuse as a survivor is Philippians 4:13, "I can do all things through Christ who strengthens me." At my weakest point when I needed someone to help me, I forgot about the Lord. Looking back it's so simple. God provides not only the wisdom but the strength to get through everything you endure through this lifetime. I could have prayed, I could have sought help from my church family because yes I still attended church. It was the unwavering foundation within my relationship with God I needed.

Without the spiritual strength, there is an internal fight that burns within victims no matter the situation...you are

The Will To Live: Finding The Strength Within To Survive

weak as a helpless baby who needs its mother for nourishment and admiration but yet trying to survive. Looking for guidance to help order your steps but when we look for someone to guide us other than ourselves we don't own it. We find ourselves going back into the abuse, blaming others for our actions, siding with the abuser, and believing there is no way out other than to continue.

You need a wakeup call whether you are being abused so severely you almost lose your life or you are tired and get fed up. It is not until you are sick and tired of being sick and tired that a change will come. In my situation, the police were called, complaints filed, and the abuser being removed from my property. Over a span of years there were black eyes, patches of hair removed, being dragged down the street, punches to the mouth, high speed chases, stalking, and death threats. While everyone looked on; sometimes helping, sometimes listening, sometimes calling the police, and sometimes breaking up a dispute. It wasn't until I was isolated in the country with a loaded gun to my head I realized I would die anyway. I either die fighting back and put an end to the domestic abuse or I die when he wanted it to happen

The Will To Live: Finding The Strength Within To Survive

on his terms. Know it's only when you are fed up and realize it's not your fault and nothing you can do will stop the abuser that your eyes are uncovered and you see the truth. You will have to leave and put an end to the abuse because this is the only way it will end. It's you with the strength and grace from God and not anyone else who can do it. Its only Y-O-U!

The Will To Live: Finding The Strength Within To Survive

Chapter 7 ~ Get the Legal System's Protection

Protection from abuse is a legal matter whether you think so or not. Any form of abuse be it verbal or physical should not be tolerated. One important thing is consistency. If no one takes you seriously they are less apt to help you. At times we aren't ready to seek legal help. We think we are; but we aren't. It becomes like a cry wolf type syndrome. When there is an incident you are fed up and go to the authorities, there's a court date, you feel bad and decide to drop the charges. All of these things come into play when using the legal system.

In an incident with my ex-spouse, I did everything right. I reported the incident by calling the police. They took a statement, I went to the doctor immediately, and I reported it to child support enforcement. Step by step, I did everything right. On my court date I presented exhibits which were filed but that still wasn't enough for the judge to approve a 2 year ex parte. It made me discouraged but I'm spiritually strong now so I still believe things would get better and I trusted God. The key here is make sure you collect indisputable facts, timelines, witnesses, and any legal documentation you can because in order for the system to work you will need it.

With the judicial system, you must persuade the judge to believe your statements and case in order to take legal action. The more consistent and documented your factual story is the easier the judge can determine the seriousness and justification for judicial action. If every time you called the police and pressed charges then went to court, it gives a legal timeline perspective of zero tolerance. Remember it is one judge's decision based on what they believe so provide as much information you can.

The Will To Live: Finding The Strength Within To Survive

Inconsistent behavior makes it easy for the other side to find issues with behaviors and your judgement in eliminating a reasonable doubt for an urgent concern. If you don't know where to start here are a few key points:

1. After an incident call authorities. This provides a time and date stamp and assist in beginning the criminal process. One thing I learned about the police statement, you must remember everything detail by detail in specificity. You must remember without any doubt what occurred, where were the placement of the hands, could you breathe? Could you not breathe? If you can't remember stick to the truth regardless of how you want justice. These details make a solid case against your abuser.

2. Remember specifics of the incidents. Make a log with notes, take pictures if you have bruises. Go to the doctor to physically document your current condition and also time and date stamp the incidents' effects on you.

3. Use advocacy groups to help you prepare your case for court. There are tons of advocacy groups

who assist with domestic violence. If you are in urgent danger and need to get an Order of Protection, they can assist in preparing you for court and tell you what to expect and also attend court with you.

4. Continue with the Order of Protection. The court will issue an emergency order if there is immediate danger. You will then be assigned a court date in which you will present your case before the judge who will make a determination as to whether an order of a longer duration is necessary.

5. Record any encounters with the abuser such as emails, calls, text messages, and place them in chronological order to be used during court or to document any incidents of concern in case you need to call the authorities because of an order violation.

6. Create a support system you can talk to and confide in. You aren't alone in this. You have people who you can depend on but most of all you must believe and depend on yourself.

When I was with my abuser, my biggest mistake was I used the system willy nilly. Sometimes I would fall for his trap and drop the charges or I felt scared. The reports I did make ended up being dropped. I remember he did a short amount of time in the county jail because the county picked up the case. It was the time when he was stalking and got dropped at my house and he took my metal weight and was going to bash my head in. Our young daughter was there so it was child endangerment and attempted assault. I remember that day which is one of many where my life was spared. My mind was so clouded with fear looking back; I could have strategically gotten out of the abusive relationship but I lacked strength. Finding the strength is easier than you think........................

The Will To Live: Finding The Strength Within To Survive

Chapter 8 ~ Disappear

Often times we want to stay close to a situation. It's hard to leave close family and friends but safety is the priority. If you are still seeing your abuser passing by or frequenting places where you may see him, you are running the risk of being in an altercation. You must carefully think through what precautions you need to take to stay safe. As you pursue justice through the system, it's going to be long sometimes, it's going to be emotional, and it's going to be draining. Your abuser can become more violent as a scare tactic to create an atmosphere of fear. Typically instilling fear may have you rethink the whole process, doubt yourself, and make excuses or be sympathetic. They can even be nice and apologetic to get you to

71

believe it won't happen again and drop the filings. These are all the things the abuser will want to happen because if convicted the abuser will have to serve the appropriate penalty for their actions.

Take this time to be focused and get your documentation and thoughts in order. If you have family or friends you can stay with it would be a good idea to do so. If you are able to take a vacation from work or work remotely that would be another suggestion. I remember when my then abuser called and threatened to blow up the office I worked in. It was a traumatic day not only for me but my coworkers as we were scared for our lives. See I knew his behaviors so when I got the call I was afraid and crying. I was able to take a leave of absence from work and hide at my Uncle and Aunt's house. It was my safe place some 60 miles away. I later was fortunate to apply for a job at a different location where I thought I would be safe.

Sometimes this may be hard to do but if you typically frequent certain shops and restaurants, distance yourself from them. Start spending time in different cities. All of these things will remove you from the

The Will To Live: Finding The Strength Within To Survive

situation and reduce your chances of running into your abuser. My mistake was I still hung around mutual friends and still went to the same establishments as my abuser. I didn't want to give that up.

Whenever there was a party or social event I was there, not realizing if I didn't go I was actually missing absolutely nothing. When you continue to frequent the same places, you have the same mindset, same patterns, and same habits. You must change your way of thinking. Do you miss your friends you used to see? Of course, but you must want something better for yourself. You must do something different if you want a different result.

One of the things which will help is to focus on goals and strategies to change your situation. The key factor is to remain focused in order to make your life better. With focus comes discipline. Discipline is what is needed to deal with abuse. You must be consistent to prepare yourself for what comes next.

73

Many times you think you should fight back due to everything you have endured. You feel hurt, upset, frustrated, and tired. Violence or revenge often crosses your mind but this is one thing that will not help your situation; it only makes it worse. Violence is never an answer because although it may make you feel good, there are laws and polices we all must abide by. Your abuser may just become more upset if your revenge plan is enacted. It could also backfire and cause you more abuse. In the worst case scenario, you would become incarcerated. You definitely don't want to lose your freedom and give your abuser that much control over your future and freedom. The best thing you can do is stay safe and protected. If this means moving, staying with friends or relatives then do so till you are able to be completely free from the abuse and the abuser has been prosecuted for their wrong doing.

I remember one instance where my abuser showed up at my apartment. It was one of his random drop offs and by the knock at the door I knew he was there to harm me. Some of the memories come in and out but what I remember was him showing up at the door. I remember my mom coming by and by the way I answered the door

The Will To Live: Finding The Strength Within To Survive

she knew something was wrong. She proceeded to call the police for me which of course angered him. What was so frustrating is I was able to make it outside and drive to the police station. But what I expected as protection from the police station, did not come.

I remember sitting in the precinct and they didn't offer anything other than the statement of, "We would advise you to go somewhere for a while." They offered me an escort to the city limits and that was it. I remember filling my car at the gas station and head about an hour away to stay with my Uncle and Aunt. I remember driving so fast before he could come to find me at the gas station, I was scared, I was saddened, and I was let down. As I sped away, I understood my abuser's reputation could allow him to get away with things he should have never been allowed. As I left my hometown, I knew again I was going to have to protect myself.

The Will To Live: Finding The Strength Within To Survive

Chapter 9 ~ You Only Live Once

When you have been abused there are a lot of emotions
which occur on a daily basis. Guilt, fear, loneliness,
shame, and hurt. All of these things allow your life to be
controlled. Your abuser feeds off of knowing they can
control you enough for these emotions to occur. The
emotions will keep you rationalizing the abuse and
continuing to endure it in fear. You live in fear that even
worse abuse will cause a physical alteration to your
appearance or maybe even death. There may be bruises,
black eyes, punches, choking, and other types of abuse.
It's not always physical, sometimes it's verbal and
emotional too. The verbal attacks on who you are as a
person, the name calling...maybe even social media

77

attacks in the hope of humiliating you in front of others. The whole point is for your abuser to make you feel devalued, belittled, and next to nothing so they can feel better about themselves. Their self-esteem depends on making themselves feel dominant, respected, and obeyed.

I learned fear early on in my experiences. The first experience was the time when I was picked up and thrown on top of the hood of a car for talking to a high school boy who had interest in me. I was 17. I still remember how it felt. I was shocked, did this just happen? While everyone watched no one said anything to my abuser, maybe they were too afraid too; who knows.

Now as I am writing this, I remember it wasn't the first time I was afraid. Maybe it was when he took my virginity in the back seat of his car. I remember it was a night where we were under a tornado watch. You could see the lightening in the sky after a mild rain. My family was at my grandpa's house for safety since we lived in a mobile home. My abuser came with his boys for what I thought was a normal visit. I would learn it would change my life.

The Will To Live: Finding The Strength Within To Survive

He threatened to kidnap me if I didn't have sex with him. I didn't believe it till I found myself on the outskirts of town. Growing up I was sheltered so maybe if I wasn't I wouldn't have been worried about his threats but I was and said, "Ok" with a sulking heart to at least get me back in town. He proceeded to turn around on the highway and headed back into town. What I remember is the parking lot at the neighborhood park. I was already in the back seat and as I said no, he was forceful and in the back seat I remember the silent tears. I remember the excruciating pain. It was horrible and painful but most important it was rape because I didn't want it! As the tears streamed down my face, that moment was the beginning of the fear. Virginity lost and raped at 17.

There were so many incidents looking back on them, some more traumatic then others but over a span of years the fear kept building and building and controlling my life. Toward the latter part I became less and less controlled and tried to get away. Those were the bad days but it could have all been avoided if I had paid attention to the signs.

The Will To Live: Finding The Strength Within To Survive

A typical weekend in Louisiana, Missouri. I was 21 by then. I would be on the social scene which mostly consisted of bars because it was a small town of 7000 or less. I had begun to get myself esteem back. I began hanging out with a local guy who was interested in me. My abuser had a hard time with this but I'm not sure why we weren't together. He cheated and although he spent his time elsewhere, no one would have me in his eyes. I belonged to him.

I was hanging out at a different spot and one of the residents got word he was coming to find me. Not knowing what to do because of the previous abuse and fear I hid in the residence. Well, he came in angry so I felt I had no choice but to come out. This was the first time I got punched in the face. The pain from the blow was one I can remember. It was the first time I saw a white light. I felt my teeth cringe and one was loose, but there was more. He drug me down the street by my hair. It was one of the worst things I had experienced and it was humiliating. He dragged me about 10-12 blocks to a friend's house I usually stayed with when I was in town. One of his friends did follow us during the dragging and begged him to stop and let me go in the car with him but that was not an option.

When we got to my friend's house, he apologized and wanted to be intimate with me. I was confused. I wanted him to leave me alone. How do you have the nerve to do this and act as if nothing happened? I wanted the abuse to stop. I wanted to be dead. I remember tons of my hair falling out from the dragging by my hair clumps and clumps along with a black eye. It was one of the tragedies I will always remember but I am blessed God brought me through. The episodes got worse. I remember I was stranded due to my car breaking down and it was winter. Again, I was in my abuser's hometown frequenting the same places and staying with the same people. It was like a scene from a movie. I went to the police station which was behind my friend's house. I needed a way to get home and back then there were no cell phones, it was the the 90s. I went to use the landline phone at the station.

My friend had a house full of people so I felt safe. As I was coming back from the station and through my friend's back door, I felt an odd feeling. A feeling that just

81

didn't seem right. Sure enough he was there outside waiting in the darkness. I ran, ran through the house trying to escape. Everyone watched doing nothing. Again he had one friend who came and told me to just go and he wouldn't hurt me. Let me remind you I was not dealing with him as a boyfriend anymore. I was doing my own thing. I was in college, trying to make a better life then what I had growing up.

So for fear of something more to come, I went out with him in the snow. I would say there as at least 3-4 inches on the ground. He took me out of the house, without any winter coat through the snowy streets. He had a tight grip so I couldn't get away. For fear of being seen, he took me down in the storm ditch full of snow. I remember my hands being cold from touching the snow and going numb because I was forced to climb in and out of the frozen storm ditch. That moment ended at his parents' house with them there. He took me to the basement and beat me with a wire hanger. This was just one of many episodes but it was after the rape at gunpoint I realized he was going to kill me either way...if I am with him or not, so I was ready to take the steps to put myself first and no longer tolerate his control and abuse.

The Will To Live: Finding The Strength Within To Survive

I decided I needed some type of protection just to help me deal with the fear I had daily because of his random popups of stalking. I was probably around 23 now and decided to get some hunting mace. After college I moved back home. I carried it around with me everywhere. It was my safety net and although it was only mace it provided me with some way of defending myself.

I remember carrying that mace around everywhere. It was my self-defense. Although I tried not to live in fear, I was scared. However, I was ready to live for me. It was over between me and my abuser. Yes, we had a child together but I was ready for his terror to end. I didn't realize he would still feel like he had some ownership as if I was property. Even though it took years, I fought my way out.

It was loving myself enough to die that I got my life back. Looking back on it, if I would have looked to God I would have gotten away way sooner. Back then I knew God but he wasn't the rock I went to In prayer during the good and the bad times. The place where I went to for counsel, guidance, and wisdom. I've corrected that

The Will To Live: Finding The Strength Within To Survive

weakness. I am now in constant prayer and am always grateful and humble for the blessings I have received even through the tragedies I have endured. See it's simple, you ask God for wisdom to know your God-given purpose in life. Once you know this purpose the storm damage on the road you are traveling is cleaned off. The bumps seem to not affect your alignment. You get better gas mileage. It is the grace and mercy of God which allows you to truly live despite what you are going through. It's all part of the story of your life where God is the author and you are reading the pages for the first time.

Chapter 10 –Loving Yourself

What is the one thing you will always have with you in your lifetime besides God? Three letters...Y...O...U...

So many things can affect you in your life from the time you are born and as you grow through elementary school to high school through your young adult years. There are ups and there are downs. You will have good times and you will have bad times. Some moments are easier than others. I truly believe a strong mind makes a strong body and what assists in your ability to overcome any adversities is your self-esteem. How you feel about

85

yourself and your individual value in any moment in time is self-worth.

With an abusive situation one must know the key to controlling you is a person's ability to belittle you to the point you lose yourself and forget the standards we have for ourselves. Sometimes guilt is a factor in allowing your worth to be diminished. You may think your actions were the cause of an abusive reaction. Maybe it was something you said...maybe it was how you acted...could it have been remnants from a lingering issue?

Being in an abusive relationship is a true test. Not only your ability to overcome but to see how much you value yourself and your well-being to not stay in the situation. I remember the days when my abuser made me feel like I was in the wrong. It's your fault, you caused it, or it's something you have done. Just the mere acts of speaking to another male giving him the indication in his head that he could lose me had nothing to do with me but his own insecurities. There were times where I was no longer under his control. He realized it so he did everything within his power to keep what control he could have and that was by any means necessary. He

86

used guilt, fear, anger, but most of all he used me to assist him in tearing me down. It was that weakness of having low self-esteem which developed from childhood caused me to think of myself as small, insignificant, and of lesser value.

Yes it's hard to find or increase your worth when there is a constant reminder be it other people or situations that condition you to think otherwise. After years have passed and I have reflected on these situations, what should I have done? One of the things was to increase the awareness of my self-worth and to capitalize on the positive things I was blessed with. An abusive situation will bring out negative things so the key to building yourself back up is finding those things which bring meaning and purpose to your life. (We will talk about purpose in the next chapter.)

During my abusive years, I was an A student, basketball star, and high achiever. I earned "first" accomplishments in my school. I still held the 400m dash record in Jr. High, became the first black high school National Honor Society President, one of the few blacks to work at the local Dairy Queen, served as an officer of Student

Council, and the most notable was to earn a full ride scholarship to college to include a paid internship. Looking back at it, why didn't I see all of these things then? In that moment I didn't see what could be. It was more of being stagnant in the negative situation, which caused a fog on all of the great things I was accomplishing. I think the fear drowned out my hopes of anything good and being able to get myself out of the abusive situation.

When I realized I was tired of being sick and tired, I got over the fear used to control me. I believed in myself and something different must come even if I died trying. It was all so easy when I reflect on it now but back then, it was so hard in the situation. I should have joined a support group. One thing I didn't do was talk to anyone. I kept everything inside and it was only until my late 30's I have talked about it and even now many do not know all or to the extent of what happened. Talking to someone can also bring you to prayer and positive energy. I had no one because I chose to stay silent due to the embarrassment. How could this have happened to me? I knew better. If I would have given myself the same love God gives to each one of us I would have been able to love myself through the abusive trials. I should have prayed more and used that time to grow closer to God. Learn the teachings of the bible so when I was in the dark those words would have helped me come to the light. I didn't pray because I was still young in my relationship with God. I loved myself but in my lowest of lows I needed inspiration, I needed a push, and I couldn't find it. In order to survive and end the abuse you have to know you have it within you.

When I do self-reflection now, positivity comes naturally. I find the good in everything. Within all the negativity I'm the shining light to so many others. This book is no different. It is about being selfless enough to share my story to inspire other and let them know if I can do it they can too.

The Will To Live: Finding The Strength Within To Survive

Chapter 11: Purpose

Purpose...what is it? It's what drives you every day. Your reason for being, which reflects what you have been put on this Earth to do. Do you know yours? Most people don't. You would be surprised how many people of various age ranges who look at me with no response when I ask this question. The majority of people wake up day after day, doing the same routine not knowing God has more for them. Life isn't about the day-to-day routines, it's bigger than that but you have to figure out just what it is If you don't know, you still have time to figure it out and truly live.

Giving your all for the ultimate purpose whatever it may be should be your main goal. Have you ever thought about the grand scheme of things? The world and everything in it? Do you think you are just here to wake up, do your routine, and continue until your life comes to an end?

Some people are goal oriented and have not only short-term goals but also long-term goals. They strive to be better and strive for success. Some are leaders and high performers you see on a regular basis but what are they chasing? Sometimes its money or status; other times gratification of doing well. They get up, work, and tend to their families if they have them day in and day out going through the motions. Many have seen their parents either driven or stuck in the routine. What is important is the sooner you find out the *why*...the easier it becomes to live.

No matter what age, it is possible to know. You must really think about it, pray, and ask for wisdom. Being consistent in trying to find out what it is will end with a wonderful discovery and that is your purpose.

No one is too young to know their purpose in life. I have three children one twenty-two and one sixteen who know what their purpose is in life and the youngest is on her way to finding hers as well. Anything which has direction will be focused and on track to achieve. When you understand your God-given purpose, you wake up every day on task knowing everything you have within you will go toward achieving that purpose.

You may ask where do I start? In order to understand your purpose you must first know what your gifts and talents are. You don't want to spend your life doing something you are not good at. Gifts and talents are the things you do well. These are those things which come easily to you and are effortless. These gifts will lead you to your purpose. Although you may see them as things you like to do, one can capitalize on their greater purpose in your life. Your gifts draw you toward your purpose and allows you to master what they mean in your life. It could be to become an advocate for the homeless, being a public servant, and things in which your work will bring people to God. Whatever your gift is, you must not waste it.

Now for me, when did I know my purpose? Was it when I was going through the abuse? No...if I had known it, it wouldn't have taken me so long to get out. As my relationship with God strengthened, I began to realize there's a rhyme to this reason. More than just waking up and going through the motions; there's a significant reason for me being here. It wasn't just to go to college, work, and make money. It's much bigger than that, but it took me until probably around my 30s that I fully knew my purpose in life; however, the understanding of it started at age 25.

I had to remove the negative clutter and drama from my life including the abuse. When you have a dark cloud surrounding you it's hard to see a peek at the sun. It started as a sense of enjoyment that I developed to possessing the key ingredients to my calling in life which consists of empowering others through my testimonies. From a weakened state to one of strength, empowerment, and overcoming through the power of God and anyone can do the same. Part of this is to be that bright shining light in the lives of so many whether it's through encouraging words, a listening ear, or providing support of their thoughts and dreams. I provide hope to those on

94

their last leg. A fresh smell of rain after a traumatic storm. I am a blessing because I'm allowing God to use me through my purpose. Even professionally to have God put me in a position to have an opportunity to touch the lives of others and make a difference is truly a blessing. In everything I do I ensure it aligns with my purpose.   I wear it day in and day out. I live to continue its everlasting power until the day I die. As I look back at the God given knowledge of my being and gifts and talents instilled within me.......it took a lot of personal growth and life lessons, but once you get it...you get it!

So I challenge you to look at your current situation as an indicator its time. Time to make a change, escape the abuse, and its toxicity on your life. If I understood my purpose and gifts; I would have been strong and not afraid. I would have been sound in my judgment and fierce in my walk of life enough to know there's a much bigger plan and not only for me but for you too.

This book is a part of my purpose. It's to use my experiences to make a difference. A difference to be the voice for so many who are broken and those of us who made it out. I first hand understand how you are feeling.

I'm also here to guide you to the end of the abuse. I'm here to show you strength and encouragement when you want to give up. It's my purpose to share intimate details of my life to make a difference and help others. I want you to know life is so much bigger than what you think. We live it not for others but for God. His love will carry you when no one is around and the love I was lacking during my days of abuse because of the dark cloud domestic violence causes. The love, strength, and purpose is right there waiting for you......you just have to see it and BELIEVE IT!

Chapter 12 - Life Lessons

How I got out is the most important part of this book. It not only freed me but is allowing me to reach back and give you what you will need to end that chapter of your life as well. One can only remain weak for so long. You realize life isn't supposed to be like this. The hurt, the pain, and the mental and physical effects are too draining. When you are tired and understand the abuse will continue to affect you, you realize I may as well die trying to get out. It's this uninterrupted dissatisfaction with your situation when one realizes you must leave by any means necessary. I am going to something greater even if I die trying.

97

I remember the day it happened for me. I had graduated from college back then, it was 1998 or 1999 and I had a family friend the same age as me who was like a sister. My home town was about 45 minutes from where she lived. I hadn't seen her and her parents in a while so I scheduled a visit. We were going to go hang out at the next town to hear the DJ. When you grow up in the country everyone knows everyone so the only DJ playing was my abuser's stepfather. My gut told me there was a chance my abuser would be there, but I wasn't under his control anymore. I was tired of being scared and not being free to live like every other human being.

To preface this moment in time, I must go back to a little in time before. While in college my abuser brought his abusive ways there. From causing a spectacle in the dormitory parking lot in front of my friends and other students, to getting dropped off in the city I went to school in. It was a continuous struggle between him coming and getting dropped off only making me call the police to get him to leave my residence. It was humiliating and embarrassing.

I would always be apprehensive when he just showed up and got dropped off with no return ride back home which was about two hours away. The most memorable thing from his consistent urge to not leave me alone was the time he had come to my apartment and tore it up. He still tried to control me and instill fear to continue the last bit of reigns he thought he had on me. So I knew to listen to my intuition because of the past and so I did this time.

Now fast forwarding to the event that freed me from my abuser. I missed and loved my friends so I felt no reason to have to be controlled any longer. I didn't expect my abuser to be at the establishment; however, my friend and her family were there to protect me if needed. I also had my hunting mace to protect myself.

So as I headed out that evening all was ok. We get to the event and had a private table with my friends and family. I was happy to be around those I've known for so long. I spoke to the DJ as I hadn't seen my abuser's stepfather in a while The night was progressing and next thing I know it was him. As my gut told me he would be there, he sure showed up. I realized at the time my only means

99

of protection was left out in the car. I told my friend and I headed outside to get it.

When we walked out to the car, I noticed my abuser looked at me and was proceeding to come outside quickly. As I hurried to the car to get the one thing I felt could save me, I had it in my hand. My abuser was then outside talking loud and calling my name to let me know I had a problem. While others were outside to watch, my friend was asking him to leave me alone and go about his business. He was loud, angry and walking toward me and my friend. When he got in my personal space, to what I assumed was to fight me, I pulled the mace out and I sprayed. Not caring.... just giving the push back I needed to do for some time now to let him know, "you no longer have control over me". In that moment I just remember spraying...spraying...and spraying until he ran off. I was free! I finally fought back and got my life back. No longer would I be subjected to his torment, intimidation, and abuse. One thing I did do was accidentally spray my friend also. I apologized as that was not my intention. Today when we talk about it we chuckle because she was there when I set myself free.

Reflecting on the last encounter where he ran away probably to alleviate the burning he had been subjected to, it was in receipt of a blessing I was able to be strong enough to realize I was ending the abuse even if I died. I remember that night—it was important and a turning point. Importantly it shows when you have nothing to lose, you must find the will to live and this instills the strength you need from within to survive these tragedies. It was that night, I did it. I WON! I fought and succeeded.

Looking back it was so easy, it was the strength I had always been looking for. I could have easily found inner strength from the Lord a long time ago but it wasn't there. God loves us no matter what and it's the same love I have for myself and others. If my relationship with God was where it was today, those signs would be enough for me. The physical punches would have never existed. All of the things that were unacceptable would have never happened because I would have been gone a long time ago.

It took years of torment to teach me some valuable lessons. These lessons I bring before you today, not to glorify the events but to help someone. We are all in this together and I believe we live our life through lessons. Some lessons are positive while others are not so positive. It's these lessons we must take something from it, learn, and grow.

I leave you with this testimony not only to touch teenage and young adolescent girls but it can reach anyone in a domestic abuse situation. We need each other when you are going through abuse. I've been there and know how you feel and what you are thinking. I will never forget it and I am here for you to lean on, to ask questions, and to confide in when you have no one else. I'm here to love you when you don't even love yourself.

I want you to use this guide for yourself, a friend, a family member, or anyone who needs a light of hope in the dimmest hour. It's when you believe in yourself to know you deserve the utmost respect and love because you were created in the image of God. He loves us with our imperfections and once you love yourself like that, all the pieces fall in place to combat abuse and your abuser.

Remember God loves you, I love you, and now it's time to love yourself.

"For God hath not given us the spirit of fear; but of power, and of love, and of a sound mind."
2 Timothy 1:7 KJV"

The Will To Live: Finding The Strength Within To Survive

Chapter 13 ~ Reach Back

When I first started this book, I thought about who is the voice for the survivors? Many on the outside state why would you do this, why would you do that; however, until you are in the situation things seem easier than they really are in the moment. I wanted to use my lessons to help someone. I want people to know they aren't alone. I've experienced it, lived through it, and I want to reach back and help others in similar situations. I'm here with you and my contact info located in the front of this book.

If you are reading this book, and know of someone, whether a friend, family member, or associate who is

The Will To Live: Finding The Strength Within To Survive

currently in a domestic violence situation, please use this to provide some support to them. One can never hear too many positive words and receive too much support. Be that support and rock they may need at this particular time. Often we feel alone due to this feeling of being ashamed of how we will be judged or perceived.

This book is meant to bring light to a dark situation. There is an end in sight and a promising meaningful life for survivors. I want you to know regardless of what you have been through, it should never define you. I've been through a lot of tragedies, but I have been very blessed by success personally and professionally. I have a very established career I've maintained for 24 years. I'm blessed to travel and have amazing experiences. I am a wonderful mother of three very outstanding young ladies. The young girl I was who had low self-esteem who was punched, drug, beaten, and broken, turned into a confident, loving, caring, beautiful spirt, and leader who found her God-given purpose in life and continues that day after day. It was my inner strength which got me through. God provided for me and kept me alive and it was for a greater purpose. I take it very seriously and not for granted.

This book is a testament to loving yourself enough to fight for the end of your abuse. The last portion of the book is sincere accounts from other survivors and one abuser who wanted to take the time to share and let you know you are not alone. These people are all special since they have been placed in my life for a reason and as I devote myself to educating, fighting, and supporting those subjected to abuse, these people are helping as well. We are here, we care, and when you need that strength look to God, yourself, and these purpose-filled words God has placed in this book to SURVIVE.

The Will To Live: Finding The Strength Within To Survive

Voices

Domestic Violence affects so many people. My accounts are unfamiliar to many people around the world. It often becomes an untold story as people may be ashamed of or are waiting for a listening ear. I wanted this book to not only be about my actual encounters but also a voice for others who are survivors of domestic violence. It not only affects women but also men.

The conclusion of this book ends with several real life experiences. These individuals wanted to share their stories to help someone overcome domestic violence and to show we all have the will survive within us if we just seek it. On story shared is that of an abuser. This unheard testimony is not to glorify abuse but give the thought pattern from that perspective. It's not to judge them but to share their lessons learned.

ALL OF THESE VOICES SHARED ARE INDIVIDUAL ACCOUNTS AND ARE NOT THE OPINION OF THE AUTHOR.

MAYUANA,
My Daughter

The earliest memories I have of my parents aren't the prettiest or warmest. I do have one memory that, for some reason, replays in my mind. A grin always seems to creep on my face as I recall it. It's a memory from a time when the leaves were changing colors and falling from the trees, creating the most beautiful scenery. I was born in Louisiana, MO. A town with a few thousand people, a Walmart, no McDonalds but what it does have is more valuable than any franchise. The beauty Mother Nature gifts this town during autumn is breathtaking! It's such a peaceful view; a narrow road taking you through the entire town in what feels like 3 miles, lined with trees of many colors, the road a rainbow of fallen leaves leading to the powerful, vast Mississippi River.

I'm not sure how old I was in this memory. I think three, maybe four. What I do remember is the leaves. They were so vibrant and colorful. I remember the crunch they made as I walked to the park using one hand to pull on my dad and the other to pull on my mom. I learned how

111

to swing that day. When I close my eyes I can still hear my dad saying, "You gotta pump your legs Pumpernickel so you can go faster." I have tears in my eyes writing this because for some reason it's a memory that's so vivid, like a picture. I don't have any pictures with my parents, just that memory. It has so much peace and warmth and love; everything that isn't what I remember of my parents. The other memories I have are a bit grimmer.

I remember the abuse. The highway car chases in the rain, the hitting, the choking, the knife to the throat, the harsh language, my mom's hysterical cries, the time she was held at gun point and my uncle had to sneak out the back door to get the cops. I remember it all. But it seems so distant now, like I don't even know those people I remember. They seem like completely different people now. But I remember. I remember being scared and being confused. I remember wondering if other kids were dealing with the same thing at home.

The experience, seeing the domestic violence involving my parents who were the age I am now, overall made me grow up. Having young parents in general makes you grow up because you witness them going from young

The Will To Live: Finding The Strength Within To Survive

adult to grown adult. The experience showed me at three and four years-old that life is not cotton candy and gumdrops.

It taught me how to be strong. It taught me how to begin preparing myself for the downfalls life has to offer. I feel like I've seen my parents at their most vulnerable moments. Vulnerable prey trying to escape a predator, vulnerable predator, angry, young and impetuous. It kind of connects us. It wasn't just them going through it, it was all of us. It affected all of us. It hurt all of us. Even to this day, I see how the three of us deal with the long term damage.

Being at the age my parents were when I was young just makes my heart yearn for what could have been. I wish that not only my mother, but my father would have had some type of asylum or refuge. Somewhere they could have retreated, talked and worked their internal problems out. That's what I hope this story, and this book can do for people. Not just the abused, but the abuser. I hope it allows all of its readers to know you're not alone, you're never alone, and it doesn't have to be this way.

You don't have to settle for loving that angry violent beau and you don't have to be that angry violent beau.

JANESSA

My life in the past 12 years has been an emotional rollercoaster. I first met him he seemed like the man of my dreams but it soon turned into a nightmare. I had my first child thinking we was in love and thinking it would last. I had my first run in: it was a smack then a punch. Calling the cops and seeing them look at me as a victim made me feel so low. Black eye and cuts on my face. I still stayed because he said sorry. Then it kept happening more and more as he became a raging drunk. I said it was time to get my daughter who was only 9 months away from him. I decided to move back home with my parents. We moved there I continued my schooling. Then I was thinking he had changed and got back with him. We had our second child and it only got worse. He would be so violent. I stayed for 2 years after that.

All the black eyes, busted lips, and bruises; I was still there, until I got up enough courage and found myself

The Will To Live: Finding The Strength Within To Survive

badly beaten and seeing that this is not love. The mental abuse was horrible: I'm fat, ugly, and so on. I would sit and cry. Almost to the point to where I have tried to commit suicide three times. Taking pills, burning myself, and cutting myself, not knowing that I should have thought about my girls. I didn't think anyone would miss me. I just thought it would take all my pain away but I was wrong. It took a lot of growing and praying to know that it's not worth it. I was not myself away from everyone I needed in my life. I came back home again and am still here to this day.

I have my own home and my kids are 10 and 8 now and doing wonderful. I have overcame my past and know that I am worth more. I have found God and now live a better life. I have many scars on me and am now in a place that I can tell my story. It has taken me over 12 years to be able to know my worth and to get right with God. I have been able to forgive him and be at peace. I can say that even though I have been abused mentally and physically I am a beautiful woman who has endured something that I never thought was possible. It can happen.

The Will To Live: Finding The Strength Within To Survive

My experience is not the worst but it has been a journey for me to get myself together. The mental abuse has to be the worse. I would always think I was not worthy of anything or anyone because of the way I was made to feel. I have learned that no one can make me feel that way, but I had to get my mind right and know that I am a strong black woman. I have to know that I have 2 beautiful girls.

Alcohol has played a big part in this and also him having seen his mother in the same situation. He went into treatment and had been in trouble. I can say that we have a friendship for our girls but I am still leery of him at times. My forgiving and forgetting are two different things. I have tried to open my heart and forgive more. It is still a journey for me and haven't told my story to many people because I was ashamed and thought it was my fault. I have learned that it was not my fault. Through the years I now know that it takes a lot of strength and prayer to overcome trials in life.

At 32, I am now going back to school and raising my girls up to know they are beautiful and queens. To be able to tell my story and know that I should not be ashamed

The Will To Live: Finding The Strength Within To Survive

makes me feel good. I am very active in my church here in my home town. I just am here as an example and trying to live right. Knowing how to forgive played a big part in being able to get my life back.

ANONYMOUS MALE

I was with a woman who in my eyes was perfect. She was tall, beautiful, funny, cool, well-educated, and easy to talk to and had her head on straight. The thing about love is it can be blinding. When I love, I love hard so there was nothing I wouldn't do for this woman. We moved in together after 6 months. They say you don't really get to know someone until you live together and that's the truth. We were friends a year before we became committed so she knew my past with women. When single I talked to and sexed multiple women. She kept that information and held onto it throughout the relationship.

The first time she accused me of doing her wrong was when she went through my phone and saw conversations with my home girl, a conversation I'd have with one of the fellas. She storms in the room with a rage as I was

117

writing music. She's yelling and screaming, I'm a calm guy so I sit there and try to explain that it's just a friend. Then out of nowhere she punches me about five times as she's yelling and crying. I'm shocked stunned and confused. I put my arms around her and she just let out a cry I never heard before. We stood there for what seemed to be an hour as she cried and apologized. We eventually went to sleep.

I asked her the next day why. She told me that's how her mom and step father argued, they fought. She told me she expected me to hit her back. She's no small woman and I'm not a small guy, we're actually the same height and at that time the same weight. She wanted a real fight, I told her I didn't grow up like that and I never seen my parents argue and I understand why but we don't have to be her parents. I remember telling her "I'll never put my hands on you" and she smiled. This same hitting situation happened three or four times more after this in a two year period.

We got engaged because I was still heavily in love. We had the same talks after each time she hit me as I held her, but by this time I told her I couldn't do this forever and we needed to get her some help. She said yes but it never happened and honestly I never pushed the issue. I also told her since we're building a family I can't have my children watch mommy hit daddy. I told her if we ever have children and you hit me I'm leaving.

My daughter is now born. She's two months old, and sleeping in the crib when I get woken up with blows to the head by my fiancé. Shocked and startled I'm wondering what's going on? She went through my phone and saw a conversation with me and one of my guy friends talking about past women. I held her but this time she didn't let me, she pushed me off and proceeded to hit me. I told her "I told you I won't do this if you hit me while we have children". She said "if you leave I'm calling the cops". I said "For them to arrest you" she said "no I'll tell them you hit me". I was confused but I left because I was the one bleeding and I was sure I had bruises.

The next day at work I was picked up by the police. I told them what happened they obviously didn't believe me. I'm 6ft and at the time I was 340 pounds, I didn't look like I was letting anybody let alone a woman beat me. I

The Will To Live: Finding The Strength Within To Survive

went to court weeks later I learned because I left they took her word over mine. I thought it was smart to remove myself from a dangerous situation. Who knows if I would be alive if I would've stayed? Sad and crazy "justice system" we have.

It took me years to trust women again. Our relationship now is co-parenting but I definitely do not trust her words. She apologized for a long time, years even but it's still a traumatic experience. I pray a lot, I trust my first instincts and never forget what I went through.

To the fellas who are going through this, you're not alone, you're not the first and sadly won't be the last. Talk to family and friends and never stay in a dangerous situation because of "love", it's not worth it. Don't be ashamed to be in this situation. Be strong and trust in yourself the good thing I got out of this was a beautiful baby girl.

RENEE CHANTEL

My husband and I purchased a house in Upper Marlboro, MD, we had a $6,000.00 + a month mortgage payment.

One morning the loan office called my phone and asked why haven't y'all paid the mortgage? I said that my husband said he paid it. A couple of days went by and she called me again, this time furious, asking why hasn't the mortgage been paid!? We had a house full of children. I stopped what I was doing, went upstairs, and asked him for his social so that I could check myself, and he complied. I went downstairs to the basement and logged in on the computer...he comes running down the steps, yelling and screaming, saying he paid the f#$#*@ mortgage. He knocks the computer off the table onto the floor and breaks the computer table wall apart. I run upstairs to the bedroom to grab my car keys, he runs behind me, when he catches up to me he grabbed me by my shirt, scratches my neck, and body slams me to the floor, which fractures my finger.

Mind you, I'm a hair stylist, and I need my hands and fingers, my livelihood depends on them. As I am jumping up off of the floor he grabs the iron foot rails on the bed and rips if off the frame, while yelling, "GET ALL OF YOUR DEAD MOTHERS S%$# OUT OF MY HOUSE B#$(@!" My mother passed two months prior. I run for the door and he runs into the next room, grabs a TV/VCR combo and throws it at me. I'm running for my life down the steps screaming and crying. All of my kids are horrified, terrified, and crying because they're seeing and hearing what is going on. I ran into the bathroom yelling "CALL THE POLICE", locked the door, and prayed with my back against the door to shield it just in case he tried to kick it in. While I was in the bathroom I could hear a bunch of shuffling and noise, he was cleaning up the debris from the broken TV.

When the police came they locked him up. We went to court the following day. What did I learn? If your kids are witnesses take them to court because the judge is human and doesn't know s$&# sometimes. The judge based his judgment on the fact that my husband sat in the courtroom all day calmly and that he can't imagine such a calm man doing anything that was described. I also feel like people need to stop abusing the court system because those of us that are telling the truth are made out to be liars. If I knew what I know now I should've seen the writing on the wall. I should've taken his rap sheet from his first wife where he copped a plea of robbery instead of kidnapping battery, vandalism, etc. which if convicted he would've served 18 years but with

The Will To Live: Finding The Strength Within To Survive

the plea he only served 4 years. The system failed me big time and I failed myself.

The day I realized I just existed in my marriage and was walking dead is the day I started fighting back.

The signs of DOMESTIC VIOLENCE that I ignored:

CONSTANT LIES: everything they say is a lie;

WITNESSES PROTECTION: you can't go anywhere without him;

ISOLATION: he wants to keep you from friends and family.

THE BREAKDOWN: they start belittling you;

WRESTLING: that lets them know they can be physical;

MANIPULATION: they change everything around to favor what they want;

THE SET UP: if y'all are out together and he will only walk three feet behind you not beside you knowing another man is going to holla at you. It's a set up for an argument or a fight with the dude;

UNEVENLY YOKED: if you celebrate holidays and he doesn't and you made that clear before marriage...he's going to make all of the holidays miserable;

RELIGION: if he preaches his religion to you, drills it in your head, doesn't follow it himself, commits adulterous

The Will To Live: Finding The Strength Within To Survive

acts over and over again, causes the family to fail and never got baptized himself. Bye Felisha;

YOUR TRUTH: doesn't exist;

CONTROL: constant arguing and telling you what to do and how to do it;

ACCUSATIONS: constantly accuses you of cheating when it's really them;

FLYING OBJECTS: always throwing things and breaking furniture;

WRECKLESS BEHAVIOR: will run you off the road, drive excessive speeds knowing it scares you, get into altercations with people and pull out a weapon with the kids present;

JEALOUS: of everything;

CLOTHING: want you to dress like a Nun;

****THEY INSTILL FEAR****

What did I learn? Pay attention people will tell you who they are in the beginning. DON'T IGNORE ANY OF THE SIGNS YOU'LL PAY FOR IT AND I PRAY NOT WITH YOUR LIFE. The 90 day rule is there for a reason, to give you time to get to know the person. It could save your life. Remember sex escalates the emotions of crazy people. It gives them a sense of closeness and entitlement. Save yourself. People only change if they want to but if they

124

are dealing with a mental imbalance only meds and counseling will stabilize them.

Think of a potential relationship like a football game. When you see the signs that's a "FLAG ON THE PLAY". Enter into any relationship with your brain and let your heart follow and if you're like me, a hopeless romantic, you have to lead with the brain or you'll end up in this situation over and over again. He got me once and I will never experience this again.

APRIL

"For I know the plans I have for you," says the LORD. They are plans for good and not for disaster, to give you a future and a hope. "Jeremiah 29:11

Boom. Boom. Boom. I can hear my heart pummeling against my petite chest, like a child begging to be let out of their crib. My thoughts all pushing violently to the front like ravenous wolves. How did I get here? What did I do wrong now? I can feel the sting of her piercing eyes scorching right thru me as she asked me in a cracking voice, "Miss Melendez, when did the domestic violence begin?"

The Will To Live: Finding The Strength Within To Survive

Beep. Beep. Beep. I wake up frantically searching for my phone to silence the brash alarm before the baby woke up. It was Sunday morning and I wanted nothing more than to get ready in peace before I would be bombarded with three children all pleading for my attention. I turn to my right and gaze at my baby girl sleeping as quiet as a mouse: I look to my left and stare at her father snoring as deafening as a bear in hibernation. I lay there and just stare at him, feeling my heart breaking as a hammer being forced to make contact with a mirror in an unrestrained swing. I lay there crying out to the Lord to please just let this man love me, please make me worthy. I fight back the tears wanting to pour out of my eyes, give him a kiss on his forehead, like every morning, and start to choose an outfit to wear for church for each of us. I usually did everything to prepare us all for the day ahead. He wakes up a few times to check his phone and get Zoe as she starts to fuss.

The services we would attend would start at 10:00 AM which gave us plenty of time to stream Pastor Steven Furtick's services while getting ready. As I am walking out the room, I hear his deep voice; "Babe, turn Elevation

The Will To Live: Finding The Strength Within To Survive

on." I back track a couple of steps and sit at the computer desk. When the light pops up from it snoozing all night, I see his email account is logged on. I see a woman's name and click on it. My hefty heart drops straight to the end of my feet. I read a conversation between him and her as they discuss how attractive they are to one another and how they miss each other. With a quick glimpse, I notice the time of the last message sent; 8:35AM January 31st, 2015. He had the audacity to lay there in bed, with my daughter and myself in the room, and have a discussion via email with another woman. I was fed up. I could feel my blood start to boil like lava in an exploding volcano. Outraged and hurt, I try and keep my composure. "Are you cheating on me again?" Looking like a deer in the headlights, he answers back. "I'm just tired of you!"

Those FIVE words caused my whole world to crumble. I grabbed my phone, walked outside and proceeded to call for help. During a call he came and snatched the phone, smashing it to pieces against the hot cement. That sunny Sunday morning had just turned to a category 5 Tornado that would further destroy and disassemble what was supposed to be a solid foundation. I stomped

The Will To Live: Finding The Strength Within To Survive

back in the house and started to pack anything and everything.

"I will not put up with this. I will not continue to be cheated on and treated like this."

Through all the yelling and him spewing poisonous words at me like venom, I try my best to remain as calm as possible. All of a sudden, I feel his strong rough hands push me on the bed in anger. I can hear his mom grab the baby. I free myself from his constricted clutch and continue to pack and wait for my help to arrive. He called the police. My sister comes and grabs the boys to take them to my mother's house about five minutes down the road; I did not want them around his anger.

The cops arrive asking question after question. I can hear the lies pouring from his lying lips as to how only the "yelling" occurred.

"I just want my daughter and then I'll leave. His mom locked her in her room. He's no good to me. He's hit me one too many times."

"Have you reported any of these incidents?"

"Well, no. I haven't. Every time we would argue he would take my phone so I couldn't call."

"Miss Melendez, I'm sorry, but there is nothing we can do. We cannot take her from him because he is the father and she is not in danger."

I wanted to die and he knew it. His smirk said it all. I waited. I sat outside his house praying that God would just give me chance to get my daughter and leave.

The plotting begins. Amie (my sister), Kourt (her friend, who had been in a similar situation) and myself sat in the car devising a plan to get my treasure. They both look back and start deliberating the plan. "I don't think I could go back in there. He's going to hit me. I don't wanna get hit again."

"You have to Ape. It's the only way. He can't take care of her. You have to be brave and go get her. We will be right here. Take this phone and leave it on. We can hear everything that will go on and if he hits you I'll go in and Kourt will call for help. You can do this. You have to."

"Ok."

I step out the car, take a deep breathe, and force my feet to step forward and walk towards the front door. Anxiety starts to pour out of my already overwhelmed brain and seep through every vein in my body. I step back in the house and sit on the couch in the living room. As they both come to have their share of attacks with their words, I sit there repeating to myself that God will make a way.

"What the f#%@ are you doing back here? You miss me? What do you want?"

"I still live here."

"You're ugly. I don't want to be with you and you're not taking my daughter. "

"April, I know your just trying to make him mad so he can hit you. You're a vindictive little snitch. And you think you're so godly."

I sit there and wait. Wait for the right time. A few minutes pass and his mom makes her way to our back bedroom after parading Zoë around as to pour more salt in my open wound. My leg shakes violently with fear. The phone vibrates against my sweaty palm,

"Where is Zoe?"

"She just took her to back room," I frantically swiped. "Are you ready?"

No. I wasn't ready. I was terrified. I knew in order to get my daughter back I would have to take a risk of being hit. It was a sacrifice and a terrifying one at that. I take a deep breathe, forced my bare feet to the floor and walked towards the dark hall leading to his back liar where my precious gold was being held captive.

"What do you want?"

"Her things my family bought for her."

"Why? You're not getting her."

I look at my baby sitting peacefully in her swing, unbuckled, and about 10 steps ahead of me. His voice gets fierce and looking up, I can see pure hatred pouring from his eyes as he tries to push me out the door way.

"Stop! Get off me!"

"Leave her alone and let her get the things" his mother says. She had only come to see what the commotion was about.

"What's going on?"

The sound of that familiar voice caught my attention in an instant. I lock eyes with Amie and time froze. With my adrenaline pumping through my veins with every quick beat of my broken heart, I rush to grab Zoe. I ran. I felt the power of his hands trying to grab me as I started running towards the door. I ran down the dark hallway, panting like a deer without water; I hear a huge thud. I hear heavy breathing and grunting from a 100 pound 5 foot 1 inch girl struggling to keep the 5 foot 11 inch, 200 pound man from grabbing me. I wanted to run back and help her but knew if I did I would lose everything, so I

The Will To Live: Finding The Strength Within To Survive

kept running. Tears covered every inch of my exhausted face. I ran out the front screen door. When my feet finally hit the street I hear Kourt say "Hurry. Get in". Right before I throw myself and my daughter in the car, he closes the door. I bent over covering my baby and I can feel the power of his anger come down in fistful blows all over. Every swing drowning out my screams to stop. I hear my sister and Kourt trying to pull me free of his grip.

"Give me the baby."

I release Zoe to the trusting hands reaching out for her. She runs in the car and speeds my treasured jewel to safety. When he realizes she is gone the pounding stops.

"Hey man, you shouldn't be hitting girls," say two men from across the street who had been witnessing the whole incident.

As I get up I see my left breast hanging in the breeze. My shirt was torn and I had been exposed. I was humiliated.

"Let's go," Amie yells.

Mustering all the strength I had left to run down the street asking for help, he grabs me by the pony tail.

"Where is she? Where is she taking Zoe?"
My silence was enough to light his fuse and with full force he swung me by my hair into his brothers silver car. The left side of my face making unwanted contact with his backseat window. We ran down the street knocking on every door and nobody wanted to help. We finally got a ride from a family around the corner and had made it safely to my mom's where I had all three of my children awaiting to be reunited with their mother. Though my body was sore and bruised, feeling the warmth of my children's kisses made the risk worth it.

After months and months of fighting in court, I was finally awarded a protective order and an order for child support as well.

I never intended to be one of those woman who get hit. That wasn't supposed to be my life. Jeremiah states that only God knows the plans he has for us and that they are good. The devil meant bad with this situation but God put down his mighty hand and fought for me to leave with my

134

baby and receive custody of her. It was because of God that not only was I able to get my daughter, but now a year later, I have attended college and I am on my fourth semester of college, I am stable in my finances, and my children need for nothing. I have had a tremendous amount of help to get me set on my feet and going down a successful path for my children. Had it not been for God's grace and mercy, I would not be here today. This story was very painful to relive but I pray that it helps others. I pray that it doesn't just help others to take themselves out of an emotional, mental, or physically abusive relationship but to also build a relationship with God. God hears our cries and when I finally let him have his way in my life at my most desperate point, I was able to see the goodness of God. I was blessed to get out when I did; others do not make it. Take heed of who you let in our life or your children's lives. Be cautious. Be careful. Be loved.

RODERICK D GRIFFITH

I've put my hands on women before in the past and have witnessed some of the author's domestic situations. As a person that has done it it's not something you just wake up and do. No man wakes up saying I'm going to beat her a$%.

There's two types of men that commit abuse. Type 1 are situations where someone is the aggressor and the other person can be viewed as intentionally provoking situations. Some women may be dealing with a man and you know he's violent and chances are if you approach him with questioning he will feel pushed and an abusive outcome arises. Type 2 are those who don't need to feel provoked. They are sadistic and don't know how to communicate with a woman other than being physical. These types never know how to treat a woman.

The author's abuser didn't charm his way into her life. It was not like she was offered to him to court. He met her from being around me as we were lifelong friends who grew up together through family. He consumed her all of her high school years and then she had a child so it was like the abuse was something normal dealing with this type of person.

A lot of the situations of abuse occurred while I was there and I felt I tried to protect her and caught many swings. As I look over the years at the two today, she is accomplished, successful, and dominate while he is still the same. She was too nice to accept a man like that. Her heart is not for an abusive man but for taking care of her children and living life. When she left she continued to progress despite her situation.

When I think about the reasons why she was abused? She was never supposed to be with him. She never deserved any of that. I feel like some people just get a kick out of the abuse.

Why didn't anyone help? The abuse went on in public at times and the police didn't do anything because they were afraid of us back then. He was surrounded by enablers who dealt with the author but didn't care enough to keep him from abusing her. He should have never been with her.

My question is was he actually envious of our friendship all of those years and did that cause some of the abuse? I grew up with her and she is one of my best female friends and I gave her this info in the hopes of telling the truth in order to help someone.

The Will To Live: Finding The Strength Within To Survive

I believe a lot of men have beat a woman. It's only the embarrassment that keeps people from knowing who has actually abused someone. All of abuse is bad but the verbal is worse than the physical. Physical abuse heals but verbal can cause you to die. A man who torments a women's mental state can cause her to think that of herself leading to the death of who she really is.

Men don't want their stories as the abuser to get out because it could affect their chances of dealing with females. I make no excuses for abuse. I'm not gonna dumb down the situation for nothing. I own up to my wrongs and I will always keep it 100.

Do I think a man that hits a woman once will do it again? He doesn't wake up thinking I'm going to beat her today. It just doesn't happen like that unless they're sadistic.

In my personal situations, the female was ready to blow up and starts asking questions poking and prodding I thought. So when you come into a situation where you already have this type of spirit and the aggressor isn't calm....things blow up. The sad thing is sometimes I felt provoked just because.

The Will To Live: Finding The Strength Within To Survive

If you are currently going through abuse, I would ask that both of you find common ground to stand on before you let your emotions and heart lead you to do something you don't want to.

SHEILA'MAE

Your present situation doesn't have to be your destination is something I hold close to my heart.

It's my lesson as a sister of someone that survived abuse. There is no way to describe what goes through your mind daily when someone you love is being abused or when a phone call of help is received. You jump up, grab a bat and start swinging. You want to fight life's battles with them and for them. At times, you shut down because you feel helpless. It seems like a no win situation at every corner. However, family members stay strong in love and support. This makes all the difference in the world. Unconditional support helps your family member. The abuser may try to control all the aspects including seclusion of the loved one from family. Tho strength inside of a person allows them to reach their purpose driven destination. It's the strength of love and reassuring a person's self-worth that matters. I would like to share words of encouragement through a poem:

Mirrored Pieces...Completeness Unveiled

All of me was supposed to be a valued gift not defined by you, but my internal DNA.

I was meant to uplift...created to soar high, yet dark nights stifled my ride.

So many years of back and forth, ups and down. I was standing in the mirror with a view on this crazy train. Daily begging and pleading to regain the sanity of all of me...I need to be whole.

Tangled in the mirror's reflective shadow was a better me. The stranger staring at me seemed so distant and unreachable to the daily touch of my fingertips. Stay focused I shouted as the mirror splintered form years of pressure.

Stay strong I whispered waiting with anticipated joy. Hope began to surround and the budding support of determination engulfed this tired spirit.

A new life from within began to shatter and defeat each jagged piece. Putting me back together again was never an option because i had always been the total package. You see my internal DNA will forever be entwined with a pattern of greatness. The gift of all of me penetrates mediocre and surpasses phenomenal.

You see it's written in my DNA code which is unmatched by another. It's my pattern sewn together that keeps me safe and secure. My cloth of self-love shields me, comforts me and challenges me.

This love is unconditionally emitted, yet omitted due to another's rage.

But like a budding sprout out of concrete I will live. This new life from within won't put back the shattered glass of old. I was never meant to be that same cracked mirror reflection.

It's a better me that has found a greatness spun totally within my fibers. No longer will this web of doubt and confusion surround. I've broken open the shell and I'm ready to fly.

All of me is free to be the unique living and loving spirit created to soar above mediocre and surpass phenomenal.

I stand before this mirrored silhouette tall and uplifted. I say boldly and with conviction....

I love you!!! I am worthy!! I am strength!! I am you now completely unveiled!

ANONYMOUS MALE

Thinking about the loving home I grew up in with my mother and father, I looked back at my life and wished I

141

could marry someone with my mother's values and views on being a mother and wife.

Being a military vet and having been to war and growing up in the roughest cities and part of NYC, even I could never call myself a victim of domestic abuse, being a male.

My story is rooted from the belief you only want to be married once and if she's good enough to have a baby by then she's good enough to marry. I wanted to provide for my child with a mother figure and my newborn with a family of love and stability. I believed my wife would want the same despite her background of being from a broken household raised by family members and step parents in an abusive household.

When you're married and living in a house with someone who shows no emotions and lacks the ability to love or be affectionate, and gives you just the bare minimum of nurturing you need to grow: you are slowly dying, I can attest to this being domestic violence, mental abuse, or battered husband syndrome.

142

Questions can be asked as to why did you stay in the marriage? It goes back to me being deep rooted in my beliefs and family values of only being married once. I felt if I showed more love then it could be reciprocated and become a learned trait; however, it only made things worse. I felt my only refuge was to show my kids that I loved them and will always provide for them despite the lack of love seen between their parents.

Counseling, therapy, and sit downs were all temporary relief which resulted in her going back to what was easiest at my expense. Back to the things she felt made her appear strong to the family who showed her no love growing up. Showing her family she was a strong Caribbean female who despite her obstacles of being raised without parents that, she made it.

In conclusion, I am now divorced and my kids grown. I have sat them down and explained my abuse and the various reasons for my lack of affection toward their mother and stepmother as well as the reason for the divorce. I can only hope and pray I have given and showed them enough love for them to have a better relationship with their partner. I've learned its best to ask

The Will To Live: Finding The Strength Within To Survive

the important questions to get to know someone before you get into a relationship with them.

I hope you appreciated this book and not only learn from it but realize, we don't have to become a product of our circumstances. We must use these events to grow, strengthen ourselves, and help others by showing them it's not about where you came from or what you have been through, it's the lessons learned and how you are able to use those lessons to help others.

This book is not for me but for all of the survivors, their families, their children's, and their future generations as we all have THE WILL TO LIVE by FINDING THE STRENGTH WITHIN TO SURVIVE!

My Words To You

If you truly know me, you know I have a thing for butterflies.....there's something about this ugly caterpillar ignored by the world as it hibernates in this unattractive chrysalis only to arise as this beautiful butterfly of various sizes, shapes, and colors all for a purpose....it's the unique wings that interest me with the patterns.......each one just as special as the next......when you go through life as a caterpillar all those things evolving within that chrysalis allow you to manifest into something special and unique and wonderfully made by God....and for that I am a butterfly!

........................Drenda Williams

The Will To Live: Finding The Strength Within To Survive

93054709R00080

Made in the USA
Columbia, SC
05 April 2018